C000098740

HORSES TO FOLLOW – FLAT 2023

Sixty-first year of publication

Contributors:
Rodney Pettinga
Richard Young

RACING POST

First published by Pitch Publishing on behalf of Racing Post, 2023

Pitch Publishing, 9 Donnington Park, 85 Birdham Road,
Chichester, West Sussex, PO20 7AJ

www.pitchpublishing.co.uk
info@pitchpublishing.co.uk
www.racingpost.com/shop

Order line: 01933 304 858

A CIP catalogue record is available for this book
from the British Library.

ISBN 9781839501401
ISSN 9771753335404

Printed and bound in Great Britain by Page Bros Group Ltd

100 WINNERS

HORSES TO FOLLOW – FLAT 2023

(ages as at 2023)

ADWAN

3 b c Oasis Dream - Triple Star (Royal Applause)

Adwan won't be the best horse that owners Al Shaqab Racing have had through their hands, but he's shown enough in three AW starts to suggest he has a future when he steps into handicap company. Richard Hannon's colt has run to a similar level of form on each of his three starts over 7f and 1m, while his reappearance third when drawn wide in a Lingfield maiden in early January was franked when the winner Mohatu went close in a handicap next time. Adwan shapes as though he'll be suited by 1m2f when he goes into handicap company (something that is backed up by parts of his pedigree) and he should be able to make the most of an opening mark in the low 70s. RICHARD HANNON

AGNES GREY (IRE)

3 b f Dandy Man - Harbour Grey (Zoffany)

Despite a starting price of 50-1 on her debut at Nottingham in October, Agnes Grey shaped with a good deal of promise to finish fourth of the 12 runners behind Jane Chapple-Hyam's progressive Save The World. Richard Fahey's filly showed her inexperience from the outset by racing keenly and she was green when asked for her effort, but she picked up nicely in the closing stages to get within striking distance of the leaders. This third foal of a 6f winner, herself a half-sister to winners at up to 1m, should come on a fair bit for the run and the form has already been franked by subsequent victories of the third, seventh, eighth and 11th. RICHARD FAHEY

AL RIFFA (FR)

3 b c Wootton Bassett - Love On My Mind (Galileo)

When this son of Wootton Bassett made his debut over 7f at the Curragh in mid-July, he was described as 'one of the picks of the paddock, a gorgeous big colt with plenty of scope.' He ran very well too, but he was green and slow to pick up, with the penny only dropping with him in the final furlong when he really came home strongly to finish less than two lengths behind Hans Anderson, who was having his second outing. A few weeks later, Al Riffa got off the mark over the same C&D – this time he settled much better and he was sent to the front with two furlongs left to run, and he quickly established a good lead, before perhaps getting a bit lonely in front. He still kept on well to win with the minimum of fuss from Salt Lake City and the race reader commented that he had 'plenty of size and has a frame to fill. He can surely only improve.' He did so in leaps and bounds as he won the Group 1 National Stakes, again at the Curragh over 7f, on his final start in September, this time beating a group of classy rivals headed by Proud and Regal, Shartash and Aesop's Fables. Hans Anderson, his conqueror two months earlier, finished over four lengths behind him on this occasion, underlining the level of improvement Al Riffa had eked out in the interim. Joseph O'Brien said afterwards: 'It was a special performance. His owners were keen to supplement him for this. It was very impressive to come from the back of the field like that. He was a big shell of a horse as a yearling and I thought he'd make a lovely three-year-old, I didn't for a minute think he'd make the two-year-old that he has made. His family is all stamina, so for him to be doing this at this stage is very positive for the future. We always thought he was a middle-distance horse, and he's closely related to an Ascot Gold Cup winner, so that's real stamina, but he's not slow. I'd imagine he's a Guineas horse for sure and we'll take it from there. He's a classy horse and very exciting.' JOSEPH O'BRIEN

ALPHA CRUCIS (IRE)

3 b g Australia - Night Fairy (Danehill)

Gary Moore is one of the best dual-purpose trainers in the game, and he seems to be able to handle any type of horse from sprinters to staying hurdlers and chasers. Although Alpha Crucis has yet to win, he's shown progressive form in three outings on turf and the AW in the autumn, and he is now one to take into handicaps. Given he's by Derby winner Australia out of a dam who won over 1m2f, the step up to 1m2f and beyond could bring about further improvement. An opening mark of 72 doesn't look beyond him, he's been gelded since his last run and he's one to look out for in run-of-the-mill handicaps in the coming months. GARY MOORE

ANCIENT RULES (IRE)
3 ch c Lope De Vega - Carriwitchet (Dubawi)

Charlie Appleby's Military Order, who had shaped well on his debut, justified short-priced favouritism at Newmarket in mid-October, but it was his stable companion Ancient Rules who gave him a bit of a scare in the closing stages and the last-named is the one to take from the race. The fact that he was at an experience disadvantage makes his performance all the more meritorious, particularly as he was green when asked to pick up by Ryan Moore inside the last half-mile. However, he gradually grasped what was required and he ran on strongly to take second place in the closing stages, shaping as though he'll be suited by the step up to 1m2f and beyond this season. That view is backed up by a quick look at the dam's side of his pedigree. The dam Carriwitchet, a Dubawi mare, is from a fine middle-distance family and Ancient Rules looks the type to make up into a smart performer in the coming months. CHARLIE APPLEBY

ANISETTE
3 b f Awtaad - Tutti Frutti (Teofilo)

An eyecatcher behind subsequent winner Tyndrum Gold in a 1m novice race at Kempton in early November, Anisette, who is a half-sister to a 1m winner, then finished second behind an odds-on shot a month later over the same course and distance, a performance which can be upgraded as she took a keen hold in the early stages. She got off the mark at the third time of asking at Wolverhampton over an extended mile in late December, where she ran out a 4l winner of a slowly run race having travelled strongly throughout. The sharp turns of Dunstall Park appeared to suit her well and she can kick on as a handicapper – she could be one note around the tight bends of Chester in early May as she encounters turf for the first time. KEVIN PHILIPPART DE FOY

ARABIAN STORM
3 b c Kingman - Arabian Queen (Dubawi)

If pedigrees are anything to go by, Arabian Storm should turn out to be a good horse this season. He's by multiple

Group 1 winner and leading sire Kingman out of the owner's Juddmonte International winner Arabian Queen, one of only two horses to get the better of Derby and Arc winner Golden Horn. The colt shaped with a good deal of promise on his racecourse debut, finding only Enfjaar too good over 7f on good-to-soft ground at Newmarket in October. It looked a highly encouraging effort at the time and the form has since been franked by next-time-out wins for the third, fourth and fifth. He's open to a good deal of improvement and he should win something similar before going on to better things. ANDREW BALDING

ARTISTIC STAR (IRE)

3 b c Galileo - Nechita (Fastnet Rock)

Maiden races at Nottingham in the autumn can often throw up a good horse or two – the 2021 Derby winner Adayar being a notable recent example – and Artistic Star looks one to follow judged on his debut win at that venue last October. The Ralph Beckett-trained colt, a brother to three winners at up to middle distances, was fairly easy to back but he turned in a very useful performance to beat Westerton, a more experienced rival, in comfortable fashion. The third home, Like A Tiger, would frank the form next time out by winning a Kempton novice over the same trip a month later. Given the way he asserted in the soft ground over the mile trip, the step up to middle distances is likely to be in Artistic Star's favour. He has no fancy entries at the moment but it doesn't take much of an imagination stretch to think he'll develop into a smart three-year-old and his reappearance is awaited with interest. RALPH BECKETT

AUGUSTE RODIN (IRE)

3 br c Deep Impact - Rhododendron (Galileo)

At the time of writing, Auguste Rodin is challenging for favouritism in the ante-post lists for the 2,000 Guineas at Newmarket in May and he is clear favourite for the Derby at Epsom in June. He ended the season as one of the best juveniles around – behind only stable companions Little Big Bear and Blackbeard in the International Classifications. Aidan O'Brien's choicely bred colt improved significantly between each of his wins. Following a convincing 7f maiden success at Naas in the summer, he made a seamless transition to Pattern company when following up in a Group 2 at

Leopardstown in September. But his best performance was reserved for the Group 1 Vertem Futurity Trophy at Doncaster in October, in which he powered clear in the closing stages to beat Epictetus and the wayward Holloway Boy in ready fashion. That win provided his trainer with a record 11th victory in the race and, given that Group 1 has a habit of producing a raft of Classic winners, it will be no surprise to see the son of Deep Impact make his mark at the highest level in the coming months. Although he has speed, stamina looks his strong suit so his best chance of Classic success could be when stepped up to the Derby (or Irish Derby) trip of 1m4f. He'll probably reappear in the 2,000 Guineas before, all being well, a trip to Epsom, and he's one to look forward to. AIDAN O'BRIEN

AUTOCRAT (IRE)

3 b c No Nay Never - Crystal Diamond (Teofilo)

Not all the well-bred Aidan O'Brien juveniles turn out to be world beaters, but every horse has his level and Autocrat, who was picked up by Denis Hogan for 42,000gns in autumn, appeals as a likely improver. The three-year-old, who wore blinkers on both his turf starts, isn't fully exposed after showing form bordering on fair in soft and heavy ground maidens in Ireland last autumn and wasn't disgraced (in cheekpieces) on his first run for his new yard on Polytrack at Dundalk in February (1m). Although easy in the market, he bettered that form when successful on his handicap debut at the same course over the extended 1m2f later in the month, off the bridle before the home turn but responding well to pressure to nose ahead in the closing stages. There's plenty of stamina on the dam's side so better can be expected granted a more truly run race over that distance or when he goes up to 1m4f and he looks ahead of the handicapper at present. DENIS HOGAN

AZURE BLUE (IRE)

4 gr f El Kabeir - Sea Of Dreams (Oasis Dream)

This grey filly had a busy time of it in 2022, running eight times in total and, while she went up 20lb in the handicap after winning four of those starts, there's every chance she still hasn't reached the ceiling of her ability. Paul Mulrennan, who was on board for two of her wins last year, said at the end of the season: 'I just knew she would become stronger physically as a three-year-old. I always knew with her, you could tell by her frame that she would fill out and make into a nice horse. I feel that she's more than capable of kicking on positively with another winter on her back. She's already a Listed winner, so Group races could be next on the agenda. She's already won at both Newmarket tracks which should offer Michael (Dods) options for next year.' The Listed race she won at HQ was the Boadicea Stakes in October and the Group 3 Abernant Stakes, which is run over the same 6f trip on the Rowley course in April, looks a logical early-season target. She may be able to progress to Group 1s after that and it's conceivable that she could also be stepped up to 7f again (she ran over the trip once at two and appeared to stay it well) and that will open up even more options for her. She's very much a filly to keep onside. MICHAEL DODS

BALTIC VOYAGE

3 b c Frankel - Baltic Duchess (Lope de Vega)

Despite remaining a maiden after four juvenile starts, Baltic Voyage appeals as the sort to win a reasonable handicap or two this season. Ralph Beckett's three-year-old, who has been gelded since his final start at Newmarket in October, showed a useful level of ability when surrounded by subsequent winners in a traditionally strong York maiden in August and he ran to a similar level at Newmarket on his final start two months later. He is a bit better than he was able to show at Newmarket, too, after getting shuffled back through the field at a crucial stage, but he saw out the 1m2f trip well, doing his best work at the finish. On pedigree, he'll be suited by the step up to 1m4f and, given he's not fully exposed, there should be a fair bit of improvement to come once his stamina is brought into play. RALPH BECKETT

BALTIMORE BOY (IRE)

4 b g Starspangledbanner - Biaraafa (Araafa)

An £85,000 yearling who didn't make the track at two, Baltimore Boy caught the eye on his belated debut at Kempton in June, where he was noted as staying on strongly in third over 7f having been forced to wait for a run. Just three weeks later he got off the mark over the same trip at Newcastle, where he showed a good attitude to get the better of three rivals who would all go on to win their next outings. Gelded afterwards, he ran with credit over 1m at Kempton in early

August, but he couldn't quite concede 6lb to Caph Star. The third home, A E Housman, who was three lengths behind Baltimore Boy, would frank the form next time by winning a Lingfield maiden. A solitary blip followed as he finished last of fourteen runners on his handicap debut at Newcastle later the same month. However, he proved that form to be all wrong as he finished a clear second off the same mark over a mile at Ascot in late September, with only course specialist Raising Sand proving too strong. He may well have won too had he not been slowly away so he did really well in the circumstances. His mark was left alone after that so he starts 2023 on an official rating of 90, which he should be able to exploit. He will probably be kept to a mile for the time being and, granted further progress, he may soon be ready to step up to Pattern class. MICHAEL BELL

BAREFOOT ANGEL (IRE)

3 b f Dark Angel - Love In The Desert (Lemon Drop Kid)

Paul Mulrennan rode more than a century of winners in 2022, his best season since 2016, and his biggest win came on this filly in the Group 3 Firth Of Clyde Stakes at Ayr in September where he produced her with a perfectly-timed run from the rear. That was just Barefoot Angel's third outing and it was a big step up from a novice she had won at Carlisle a few weeks earlier. Oisin Orr rode her on her final start of the season in the Two-Year-Old Trophy at Redcar and she ran another fantastic race to finish fourth behind Cold Case. She looked to be struggling 2f out but she kept on strongly thereafter to be nearest at the finish. She's a sister to a 7f winner and she promises to do even better when stepped up to that sort of trip at three - she's definitely one to remain interested in. RICHARD FAHEY

BAY BRIDGE

5 b c New Bay - Hayyona (Multiplex)

There aren't many better trainers around than Sir Michael Stoute when it comes to nurturing a late-developing type. The most recent example of this has been his handling of Bay Bridge, who broke through to the top table last season. In typical Stoute fashion, he'd been brought along steadily during his three-year-old career in 2021 - a season that resulted in four wins from as many starts - but he looked an improved performer on his reappearance last year when thrashing short-priced favourite Mostahdaf in the Brigadier Gerard at Sandown in May. A combination of quick ground and a slow pace conspired to get this heavy-topped sort beaten in the Prince Of Wales's Stakes at Royal Ascot and he was below his best behind Vadeni in a muddling Coral Eclipse back at Sandown in early July. However, he confirmed he's one of the best around with his defeat of last year's Derby winner Adayar in the Qipco Champion Stakes on good-to-soft ground in October, with the hitherto unbeaten Baaeed having to settle for fourth place. Given his physique, there's every chance he could progress again from four to five and there's enough in his pedigree to suggest he should stay 1m4f. It wouldn't be a surprise to see him being campaigned abroad at some point and he's one to look forward to this year. SIR MICHAEL STOUTE

BOPEDRO (FR)

7 b g Pedro The Great - Breizh Touch (Country Reel)

David O'Meara made his mark in some of the better-class handicaps last season, as demonstrated by the wins of Orbaan in the Golden Mile handicap at Glorious Goodwood and Summerghand in the Ayr Gold Cup. He has another one in the shape of Bopedro that could pay his way in some of the more valuable handicaps judged on the form he showed in five starts for O'Meara in 2022. This multiple winner in France and Ireland is effective over both 7f and 1m and he's on a good mark at present compared to the pick of his form for Jessica Harrington that saw him rated 107 at his peak. He handles most ground and, given that his two best efforts last season were over the straight mile at Ascot and over 7f at Doncaster, he makes each-way appeal at decent odds if lining up for the Lincoln Handicap at Doncaster in early April. DAVID O'MEARA

CAIRO (IRE)

3 b c Quality Road - Cuff (Galileo)

Cairo's juvenile career was all about improvement and he's the type to add to his tally of two wins in the coming season. Aidan O'Brien's colt didn't see the track until early August, but he more than confirmed his debut promise over 6f when justifying his place in the market upped to 1m at the Curragh at the end of the same month. A Listed second placing on his AW debut at Dundalk in late September bolstered the view he was still on the upgrade and he turned in his best effort on this final start when winning at Group 3 over 7f at Leopardstown in October. That form has already been advertised by the subsequent wins of the runner-up and the seventh, and the stable's representative said afterwards: 'he's a lovely horse physically and he's done everything right so far.' What his best trip will be remains to be seen but it'll be a surprise if he's asked to go further than 1m2f. AIDAN O'BRIEN

CANNON ROCK

3 b g Fastnet Rock - Fintry (Shamardal)

Although disappointing when green on his debut at Leicester in October, Cannon Rock was a different proposition over quarter of a mile further at Newmarket a fortnight later. Fitted with cheekpieces, he showed much-improved form to beat the 82-rated Sir Laurence Graff by three quarters of a length, the pair pulling clear of the remainder. Charlie Appleby had taken the same race the previous year with St Leger runner-up New London and, while he has some way to go before he reaches the achievements of that one, he's certainly a promising sort. Judged on that win he should have no problems with 1m4f, he's open to plenty of improvement and he might be able to win in handicap company before stepping up in grade. CHARLIE APPLEBY

CHALDEAN

3 ch c Frankel - Suelita (Dutch Art)

Andrew Balding won his first 2,000 Guineas in eerie silence in 2020 with Kameko and the atmosphere at Newmarket will surely be very different should Chaldean be able to win it for him again with Frankie Dettori on board this May. A son of Frankel out of a Dutch Art mare, Chaldean made a pleasing enough start to his career at Newbury (6f) in June, finishing fifth of 13 behind Seductive Power after keeping on well in the final furlong. His trainer, who clearly already held him in very high regard, was perhaps a little underwhelmed by that performance, but he didn't look back after that. He got off the mark over 7f back at Newbury a few weeks later and that form worked out very well with the next three home all winning next time out. Chaldean himself won the Group 3 Acomb Stakes at York in August, in which he displayed a willing attitude after racing keenly to see off Indestructible, with the rest of the field well beaten off. He was able to confirm that form in September in the Group 2 Champagne Stakes, again over 7f, but this time he put three and a half lengths between himself and the same rival, with the soft ground at Doncaster not bothering him at all. His final assignment was the Group 1 Dewhurst Stakes at Newmarket in early October, and he came through it with flying colours, holding off the fast-finishing Royal Scotsman, with the likes of Nostrum and Aesop's Fables further back. Andrew Balding confirmed that the 2,000 Guineas was the next aim: 'He will be fine [in a Guineas] and the bigger the field the better off he will be. He is all speed on his dam side out of a Dutch Art mare and I'd be surprised if he got further than a mile. I don't know yet if we run him in a trial first, we'll see how he is training in the spring and make a decision there.' ANDREW BALDING

CHESSPIECE

3 b c Nathaniel - Royal Solitaire (Shamardal)

Simon and Ed Crisford sent out 85 winners from their Gainsborough Stables base in Newmarket in 2022 at an impressive strike-rate of just over 23 per cent and that total included two Group 2s and four Group 3s. One horse who could add to that impressive tally in 2023 is this son of Nathaniel out of a Group 2-winning mare, who gave the impression that he would be worth following when winning a 1m2f Newcastle maiden on his only start in November. He won with relatively little fuss, racing prominently throughout, taking it up over a furlong out and then seeing off the challenges from Hadrianus and Humanity as they tried to lay it down to him in the closing stages. The runner-up franked the form by winning a similar event at Kempton over slightly further a month later. Ed Crisford said afterwards: 'We're very pleased with this win and he'll be an exciting prospect for next year. We'll put him away now and let him strengthen and see where we go next spring.' He's bred to stay middle distances and he could go to the top. SIMON & ED CRISFORD

COLTRANE (IRE)

6 b g Mastercraftsman - Promise Me (Montjeu)

Coltrane really came of age last season, which saw him improve to the tune of 20lb in a fairly busy campaign.

Although he was touched off by the unexposed Cleveland in the Chester Cup, he quickly made amends with victory in the Ascot Stakes, where he showed ability and guts in equal measure to fend off two Irish challengers in the closing stages. A Listed race quickly followed and he again showed all his qualities when winning the Doncaster Cup in September, a race in which he outbattled leading stayer Trueshan, who admittedly was a bit below his best. Andrew Balding's runner failed to confirm placings with that rival in the Long Distance Cup at Ascot on Champions day, but his head second (clear of the rest) still represented a career-best effort. He wasn't seen out again but, if he can improve again over the winter, he'll be a force in all the Cup races next year. The Dubai Gold Cup over 2m at Meydan on World Cup night might be a good starting point. ANDREW BALDING

COME TOGETHER (IRE)

3 b g Gleneagles - Zut Alors (Pivotal)

A half-brother to six winners including Baccarat, Precieuse and Peut Etre, Come Together was a big eyecatcher on his debut over 7f at Salisbury in late September. Slowly away and carried right as they left the stalls, he ran green but he stayed on with real purpose late on to finish sixth of 12. His next start at Doncaster in October was a bit of a damp squib as he finished ninth of 13 runners but the heavy ground at Town Moor clearly didn't play to his strengths at all. He was able to show his true colours on his final start of 2022 at Wolverhampton in November, where he won a 1m142y novice stakes, in which he ran on strongly late on to get the better of the Simon and Ed Crisford-trained Intricacy, who franked the form a few weeks later by winning a similar race over the same C&D. Come Together was awarded an official rating of 85 after that performance and it is a mark he may well be able to exploit in handicaps at up to 1m2f before hopefully going on to better things. RALPH BECKETT

CORYMBOSA

3 b f Frankel - Diamond Fields (Fastnet Rock)

At this stage Corymbosa is more about potential than proven form, but she showed a fair bit of ability on her debut at Kempton in November and she appeals as the sort to raise her game in 2023. Sir Michael Stoute's filly, who is closely related to a 1m2f Group 3 winner, didn't have the pace to trouble the leaders on that debut run but the race, won by Dancing Goddess, is worth keeping an eye on given the two that finished immediately ahead of Corymbosa both won next time, while the ninth has also won since. A step up to 1m2f should be in her favour and, while she might be vulnerable against the better sorts in this type of event, she'll be one to keep an eye on when she goes handicapping. SIR MICHAEL STOUTE

DENSETSU (IRE)

3 b f Gleneagles - Zenara (Sea The Stars)

Densetsu is unlikely to be anything out of the ordinary but she's shown ability on turf and the AW and she's the type to win more races. Marco Botti's filly shaped well on her debut over 7f at Newmarket behind Mammas Girl (who also makes it into these pages) and showed a bit of improvement when getting up in the closing stages to beat subsequent winner Outrace on AW at Wolverhampton in late January. She is a bit better than the bare facts of that win given she came wide and only hit the front in the last few strides. Although beaten at Lingfield the following month (1m2f), there's enough in her pedigree to think that she should prove fully effective over 1m4f and she should pick up another handicap or two. MARCO BOTTI

DESIGNER

4 ch f Pearl Secret - Curly Come Home (Notnowcato)

Although Designer has won three of her 11 career starts, her best effort on ratings came in defeat on her most recent outing when she finished second on heavy ground at Doncaster over 5f in November and she's one to bear in mind for a good-quality handicap this time around. The filly won two of her seven starts in 2022 – at Kempton on her reappearance in the spring and a fillies' handicap at York's Ebor meeting in August and she's already shown that she's effective on ground ranging from good to firm to heavy. Granted a bit more improvement, it wouldn't be a surprise to see her taking her chance again in minor Group company and, although she's only raced over sprint distances since her debut, her pedigree – her dam won twice over 1m2f and over an extended 1m3f – suggests she's well worth another try over 7f. The dam Curly Come Home showed her best form as a four-year-old and it's not beyond the realms of possibility that her daughter will follow suit. JOHN BUTLER

DIVYA (IRE)

3 b f Galileo - Nahema (Dubawi)

Although Divya was a disappointing 7-2 second favourite at Haydock on her second start in late September, she showed more than enough on her other two outings flanking that below-par effort to suggest that she's up to winning races this term. A daughter of Galileo from a fine middle-distance family, Divya showed fair form on her debut over 1m at Ascot in early September and also when third to Cannon Rock (another of the 'hundred') when upped to 1m2f in a Newmarket maiden on her final start in mid-October. She's open to further improvement and her pedigree suggests that she will be well suited by a step up to 1m4f and beyond. She should be able to make her mark in ordinary maiden or novice company before going into handicaps and, with a pedigree like the one she possesses, the aim will no doubt be to get her some Black Type as the season progresses. ED WALKER

DRAMATISED (IRE)

3 b f Showcasing - Katie's Diamond (Turtle Bowl)

A daughter of Katie's Diamond, who was a Listed winner for Karl Burke over 6f in 2015, Dramatised made a huge impression when winning a 5f maiden at Newmarket in late April, where she put clear daylight between herself and seven rivals, headed by Malrescia, who went on to win her next two starts. The time was decent too, and she duly confirmed that initial promise by running out an impressive winner of the Group 2 Queen Mary Stakes at Royal Ascot on just her second start in June, despite her rider dropping his whip inside the final furlong. It was thought that a step up to 6f wouldn't be a problem for her, but she came unstuck over that trip on her next start in the Lowther Stakes at York, where she raced keenly under her penalty, eventually giving way in the closing stages to finish a well-beaten fifth behind her stablemate Swingalong. Nearly three months later, Dramatised was sent to Keeneland to contest the Breeders' Cup Juvenile Turf Sprint over five and a half furlongs and, despite playing up in the preliminaries and negative market vibes beforehand, she ran really well to finish second to Mischief Magic, a 6f specialist, who took full advantage after

Dramatised found herself in front sooner than ideal. Clearly, a return to 5f will help in the short term and, as she learns to relax in her races, she will give herself a decent chance to prove herself at 6f in time. It would be no surprise to see her win a Group 1 in 2023. KARL BURKE

ELECTRIC EYES (IRE)

3 b f Siyouni - Love Is Blindness (Sir Percy)

A 45,000gns yearling out of an unraced half-sister to French Derby winner Reliable Man, Electric Eyes made a winning debut in an ordinary 7f novice on soft at Thirsk at the start of September. Bred to stay further, she got outpaced as the race began in earnest but she responded well to pressure to eventually prevail in a three-way tussle with Spirit Of Applause and Three Yorkshireman, with that trio pulling a long way clear of the rest. Just three weeks later she was asked to contest the Group 2 Rockfel Stakes over the same trip at Newmarket and she didn't disappoint, finishing a gallant second to the classy Commissioning, beaten by two and three quarter lengths on good ground. Her trainer said afterwards: 'We were a little bit further back than ideal and if we'd been tracking the winner I think we'd have given her a real race.' At that stage there was talk of her being supplemented for the Fillies' Mile which Commissioning would go on to win just over two weeks later, but those plans were ultimately shelved. A step up in trip now beckons and she could turn out to be a Group-class filly at around 1m2f as she resumes her career. KARL BURKE

EMPRESS WU

3 b f Sea The Moon - Chinoiseries (Archipenko)

Raceform's race reader described this filly as 'potentially Pattern class' after she won her only start as a juvenile, a 1m2f maiden on Lingfield's Polytrack surface, in mid-November. Sent off at 16-1, she was held up towards the rear after being steadied at the start by rider Jim Crowley, but she made smooth headway to get into contention on the home turn and, after being switched right over a furlong out, she displayed an impressive turn of foot to coast home by two and a quarter lengths. Owned and bred by Kirsten Rausing, she's out of a sister to 1m4f Group 1 winner Madame Chiang and she's a filly to look forward to as she returns to action in the spring. DAVID SIMCOCK

EPICTETUS (IRE)

3 b c Kingman - Thistle Bird (Selkirk)

This English/Irish Derby entry raced three times as a juvenile and improved every time with the promise of more to come from him at three. The 7f maiden, which he won on debut in July at Newmarket, was strong form, with plenty of the beaten horses, including Desert Order, Flying Honours and Signcastle City, winning subsequently. John Gosden said afterwards: 'Epictetus wasn't fully wound up for the race and we have to be absolutely overjoyed with him.' He wasn't seen again until October when contesting the Group 3 Autumn Stakes over 1m on the Rowley course at Newmarket. He ran another fine race, narrowly losing out to Silver Knott, who was having his fifth start, with the Chesham winner Holloway Boy over two lengths away in third. He was well backed beforehand and it was probably the winner's experience that was the deciding factor. His final assignment was the Group 1 Vertem Futurity Trophy at Doncaster two weeks later and it proved something of a strange contest. Racing on heavy ground, they split into two groups, with Epictetus joining two Ballydoyle horses, Auguste Rodin and Salt Lake City, in a trio that raced on the near side, while the rest of the field ran on the opposite flank. Epictetus ran a great race, finishing second behind Auguste Rodin, beaten by three and a half lengths, with a further two lengths back to his old adversary Holloway Boy, who had drifted right across the track. He was a bit short of room inside the final furlong, thanks to Holloway Boy's antics, which probably affected the winning margin but not the result. John Gosden was upbeat afterwards: 'Epictetus has run great. He's still an immature horse, he's still on the weak side and the ground found him out but he's a grand horse for next year. We'll start him out at a mile and a quarter in a trial, something like the Dante.' On breeding he is not absolutely guaranteed to stay the Derby trip, but he may well prove to be Frankie Dettori's final ride in that great race should he come through his trial okay. JOHN & THADY GOSDEN

EXPELLIARMUS (IRE)

3 b f Churchill - Gilded Reflection (Zoffany)

Expelliarmus is named after a disarming charm in the Harry Potter books that forced whatever an opponent was holding to fly out of their hand. Ironically, the rider of the equine version actually dropped his whip in the last half of the race, but it probably made little difference to the outcome judged on her ninth of 14 placing on heavy ground at the Curragh on her debut in late October. Nevertheless, the filly did hint at ability and she should come on a fair bit for that initial experience. She's closely related to a 1m4f Flat winner who also won over hurdles so a good test of stamina is likely to be required and she's one to keep an eye out for in modest company when she ventures into handicaps. She's in good hands and it will be a surprise if she doesn't leave these bare facts well behind at some stage. JOSEPH O'BRIEN

FEUD

3 b g Dubawi - Agnes Stewart (Lawman)

Not every horse in this 100 can go on to be a future Classic winner and that comment certainly applies to Feud, but he showed enough ability in three runs last season to suggest that there are handicaps to be won with him as he resumes his career. A half-brother to Divine Jewel, who has shown ability over 1m4f+ for Roger Varian, Feud made his debut over 7f at Newbury in September and it was a satisfactory introduction as he finished fourth of 15, gradually weakening out of contention in the final furlong. He confirmed the promise of that run a few weeks later at York over a mile. Taking a while to get going in the straight, he worked his way into contention before his run flattened out towards the finish, but third place of the 12 runners was still a decent showing. He was disappointing in the context of that run on his final start of the year at Kempton in November, again over a mile, finishing seventh of the 13 runners after weakening over one furlong out. However, it later emerged that he had an abnormal scope, so perhaps a line should be drawn through that run. He was gelded after that final run and is likely to come into his own in handicaps over 1m2f+ at three. He remains one to be interested in. RALPH BECKETT

FIVE TOWNS

3 b f Lord Kanaloa - Guilty Twelve (Giant's Causeway)

Five Towns is a typical William Haggas horse who has improved with racing and she's one to take into handicaps on the back of a juvenile career that saw her get off the mark at the third attempt in a Kempton novice event over 7f in October. That day, she improved to the tune of 12lb using Racing Post Ratings as a guide and there's likely a fair bit more in the way of progress to come this year. Given she's a half-sister to Three Priests, who won over just shy of 1m4f and is out of a dam who won over 1m3f in the US, the step up to 1m2f and beyond should be very much to her liking. It's not clear at this stage whether Five Towns's improvement in October came about as a result of her switching to an AW surface for the first time or the fact that she is just getting better as she matures but, whichever scenario proves correct, she looks certain to take advantage of an opening mark of 78, which should give her plenty of options in handicaps. WILLIAM HAGGAS

FLYING HONOURS

3 b c Sea The Stars - Powder Snow (Dubawi)

Flying Honours ended his juvenile career with victory in the Group 3 Zetland Stakes over 1m2f at Newmarket in October and he looks a decent middle-distance/staying prospect for 2023. Charlie Appleby again has strength-in-depth in abundance in the three-year-old department and his colt, who had five races last year, is very much the type to raise his game again this time round. In fact, everything about his profile and his pedigree suggests he could develop into a St Leger type granted normal improvement. He doesn't have a Derby entry (though he could be supplemented) and a suitable target for the first half of the season could be the Group 2 Queen's Vase at Royal Ascot over 1m 6f, a race his trainer won with Kemari in 2021. He's only raced on a sound surface so far, although his pedigree suggests he should prove equally effective on easier ground given that his dam posted her best effort when winning a heavy-ground Listed event in France. There's plenty to like about him. CHARLIE APPLEBY

GREEK ORDER

3 b c Kingman - Trojan Queen (Empire Maker)

A glance at his pedigree shows that Greek Order is a full brother to Listed and Group 3 winner Sangarius, who won a Group 3 over 1m2f for Sir Michael Stoute as a three-year-old in 2019. Although he has a way to go before he can match the achievements of that sibling, Greek Order showed enough in two starts as a juvenile to suggest that he can win in novice company before going on to compete in some of the better handicaps. He'd clearly been working well at home prior to his debut, where he started at 6-4 favourite at Salisbury (7f) in September and, although he didn't win, he ran well in third place – ahead of three subsequent AW winners. He again started at 6-4 for his next start at Newmarket, again over 7f, with Ryan Moore in the saddle, and he stepped up slightly on that form on quicker ground by finishing a neck second to Charlie Appleby's Regal Honour, the pair pulling a few lengths clear of the rest. He should be suited by the step up to 1m and beyond and it will be interesting to see how he progresses this year. HARRY & ROGER CHARLTON

HARRY'S HALO (IRE)

3 ch g Harry Angel - Postale (Zamindar)

Juvenile winners wouldn't really be Kevin Frost's speciality, so it's highly encouraging that Harry's Halo was able to win twice as a two-year-old in 2022. His first two starts at Doncaster and Pontefract suggested he'd struggle in maiden or novice company, but he was gelded soon afterwards and showed marked improvement to win his third career start back at Pontefract in October. Heavy ground was an unknown for his final outing at Doncaster on November Handicap day, but he turned in his best effort by beating reliable yardstick and subsequent AW winner Danger Alert by a length. Although not seen since, he's the type on looks who will improve physically with a winter on his back and there's enough in his pedigree to think that he will be fully effective over 7f when the time comes. He'll likely be no world-beater but it'll be a surprise if he doesn't add to his tally this year. KEVIN FROST

HASKOY

4 b f Golden Horn - Natavia (Nathaniel)

A daughter of a 1m2f Listed winner by Derby winner Golden Horn, Haskoy could not have been more impressive on her belated debut at Wolverhampton in late July, as she ran out a 7l winner of a 1m4f novice stakes, with the runner-up Jahoori franking the form next time by winning comfortably over the same trip at Ffos Las. Haskoy's next assignment was a big step up in grade as she contested the Listed Galtres Stakes at York but she proved up to the task as she overcame greenness to pull clear of the field with Time Lock, who finished a neck behind her. She was supplemented for the St Leger at a cost of £50,000 after that, but she ran another cracker to finish second past the post behind Eldar Eldarov, despite again racing keenly and hanging late on, which resulted in her hampering Giavellotto. The stewards demoted her to one place behind that rival so the form book shows her finishing fourth, but she emerges with plenty of credit. A tilt at the Prix Royal Oak at the Arc meeting was shelved and she was put away for the year, but her return to action is eagerly awaited as there is still plenty of untapped potential to be unearthed. RALPH BECKETT

ICONIC MOMENT (IRE)

3 b c Harry Angel - Purplest (Iffraaj)

This 41,000gns son of Harry Angel did plenty wrong on his debut at Chelmsford over 7f in October – he missed the break before coming through to lead over 1f out and he then ran green before swerving left in the closing stages – but he still prevailed fairly comfortably at the finish. The race reader commented: 'He should be much wiser for the run and looks a fair prospect.' Two weeks later he ran over the same course and distance and this time he looked a different proposition, saving ground on the inner throughout before quickening to lead over 1f out and then going clear to defy his penalty with ease. A big, strong-looking colt, no firm plans were outlined for him after the race but he's clearly got loads of ability and there are some nice races to be won with him at three. JAMES TATE

IMPERIAL EMPEROR (IRE)

3 b c Dubawi - Zukhova (Fastnet Rock)

Charlie Appleby had a stellar year with his juveniles in 2022, resulting in 63 winners at a strike-rate of 38 per cent and that tally includes nine Group/Graded winners, including two Grade 1s. Imperial Emperor, a brother to the yard's First Ruler, who won twice as a three-year-old in 2022 (1m/1m2f), only ran once in 2022 but it was a winning debut which suggests he has serious potential over middle distances this season. A sizeable individual with plenty of scope, he showed signs of greenness in the 1m Newmarket maiden he contested at the start of October, but he got better the further they went and he won easing down by three and a half lengths from the William Haggas-trained Attaj. Appleby said afterwards: 'Imperial Emperor is a nice horse with a lovely pedigree. He's a proper mile and a half horse for next year. We came up here with the confidence that he was going to run a nice race and he has duly obliged.' He was put away after that run with this season in mind, and he's one of many that the trainer can look forward to. CHARLIE APPLEBY

INFINITE COSMOS (IRE)

3 ch f Sea The Stars - Waila (Notnowcato)

A half-sister to a 9.5f AW winner also trained by Sir Michael Stoute, Infinite Cosmos created a good impression on her sole two-year-old start at Doncaster in October, which augurs well for her as she starts tackling middle distances at three. Slowly away in a fair-looking fillies' maiden over 1m, she made steady headway from about 3f out before keeping on pleasingly in the closing stages to finish within a short head of the Andrew Balding-trained Sea Of Roses, who was having her second start. In a slowly run contest she did well to make up so much ground and the front pair finished well clear of the remainder. She should win her maiden over the same trip or slightly further as she returns to the track in the spring and she can then go up in grade and distance as the season progresses. SIR MICHAEL STOUTE

ISRAR

4 b c Muhaarar - Taghrooda (Sea The Stars)

Although Israr bombed out on his final start of 2022 on very deep ground in the November handicap, that run could have come too quickly after his winning effort on a similar surface (also at Doncaster) the previous month and he's well worth another chance this term. In fact, he appeals as the sort who could turn into a player in a race like the Ebor – a race in which John Gosden won with Muntahaa in 2018 and the yard (John & Thady) won last year with Trawlerman. Heavy ground looked a concern at Doncaster in October but the progressive four-year-old quickly dispelled the notion that he couldn't act on it when beating Sir Rumi by nearly four lengths, with the rest of the field well spaced out. Whether he's asked to race on that sort of terrain again remains to be seen but he's fully effective on quicker ground and, if he shows up well in the Ebor, a trip to the Melbourne Cup might not be out of the question. He's a smart sort with a good cruising speed who isn't fully exposed after only eight outings and, although he's yet to race in Pattern company, he won't have to improve too much to justify a place in such a line-up. JOHN & THADY GOSDEN

KING OF STEEL (USA)
3 gr c Wootton Bassett - Eldacar (Verglas)

It says plenty for the regard in which King Of Steel is held that he was allowed to take his chance in the Group 1 Vertem Futurity Trophy at Doncaster in October on only his second racecourse start. Although he didn't figure in that contest after racing on the opposite side of the track to the principals, he's a grand sort on looks and just the type to make his mark at a more realistic level this season. Although he has an American pedigree, he made light of the soft ground at Nottingham on his debut, travelling strongly and pulling clear in the closing stages to beat a Sir Michael Stoute-trained runner (who had the benefit of previous experience) by nearly five lengths. In the circumstances it was a bit of an ask to expect him to follow up, stepping up markedly in grade only ten days later at Doncaster on even more testing ground. He failed to get involved after again racing with the choke out – something that connections will have to address before the coming season – but it's early days yet and, given that he's open to plenty of improvement, he could easily develop into a smart sort in the coming months if he learns to settle. DAVID LOUGHNANE

LA YAKEL
4 b g Time Test - Tebee's Oasis (Oasis Dream)

The step up to middle distances proved key to La Yakel's improvement last season, and he's just the type to make further progress this time round. Although beaten over 1m at Nottingham and at Windsor on his first two starts in May and June, he got off the mark on his AW debut upped to 1m3f at Southwell in July. He was faced with a sterner test on his handicap debut back on grass just over a month later, but he turned in his best effort to follow up at Ascot (good to soft) in a race that was franked by the subsequent wins of the fourth and sixth. Although beaten back on a sound surface over 1m4f at Newmarket on his final start of 2022, he's only had five runs and looks just the sort to develop into a smart handicapper this term for his excellent trainer. A stamina test will suit him and, although he seems to handle a sound surface, he may well be ideally suited by a bit of give underfoot. He's still unexposed and there could be a decent handicap in him either over 1m4f or over 1m6f. WILLIAM HAGGAS

LADY MOJITO (IRE)

3 b f Kessaar - Smart Bounty (Bahamian Bounty)

A £37,000 breeze-up purchase who is a half-sister to Quiet Waters and Trixie Waterbury, Lady Mojito did best of the newcomers when finishing third of ten runners behind Mystic Pearl at Thirsk in a 7f novice stakes in September. The race reader felt that it was purely a lack of experience that prevented her from going through with her finishing effort and she was noted as a likely winner next time. She duly did get off the mark a month later in a similar race at Redcar, but the authority with which she won suggests she has a bright future. Making all against the favoured far rail, she scooted away from her rivals to score by five and a half lengths from Maltese Falcon with daylight back to the rest. Richard Fahey commented: 'She is progressive and a filly we like. I thought she ran well first time and she's improved. I don't know what she beat and she was probably helped by going over to the far side.' It's fair to say that the form has yet to be fully tested but there's no doubting her potential and she's a nice prospect. There's no obvious stamina in her pedigree so she will probably be kept to similar trips in the short term. RICHARD FAHEY

LAUREL

4 b f Kingman - Promising Lead (Danehill)

A daughter of Kingman with plenty of winners in her pedigree, Laurel was well backed before her debut in a 1m fillies' novice at Newmarket in late July even though she faced a rival with some decent form already in the book. The fact that she was able to dispatch that 95-rated rival, Mashaaer, by 3l despite having to wait for some room against the rail, did suggest she was a filly of some potential. She looked equally impressive when easily seeing off Pure Dignity and One Morning, both winners of their most recent starts, in another fillies' novice at Kempton two months later and, following that run it was decided that she should be supplemented for the Group 1 Sun Chariot Stakes at Newmarket, again over

1m, at the start of October. She rewarded that confidence by finishing second of the nine runners, three quarters of a length behind the winner Fonteyn, who had a big experience edge on her. In fact, it was probably the lack of experience that cost Laurel the win as she looked to have the race at her mercy as they entered the final furlong, only to get outbattled in the run to the line. John Gosden was philosophical afterwards: 'Quite frankly, Laurel has never been off the bridle in her life and was a bit confused as to what was required, but she has run a massive race in her first Group 1.' That win at the highest level will surely come at four, either over 1m or 1m2f (her dam was a Group 1 winner of that trip at four) and races like the Falmouth Stakes, Nassau Stakes and the Prix Jacques Le Marois all look suitable targets. JOHN & THADY GOSDEN

LEZOO

3 b f Zoustar - Roger Sez (Red Clubs)

When a trainer of the calibre of Ralph Beckett says 'We haven't had one as good as this at this stage' you sit up and take notice – that is exactly what he said after Lezoo won the Group 1 Cheveley Park Stakes over 6f at Newmarket in late September in which she eased clear from a strong field, led by Meditate. The runner-up went on to win the Breeders' Cup Juvenile Turf by a wide margin on her next start, while the third and fourth, Mawj and Swingalong, had both already won Group 2 races earlier in the season, so there is no doubting the validity of the form. Mawj was, in fact, the only horse to beat Lezoo all season and that came in a muddling Duchess Of Cambridge Stakes at Newmarket in July, in which the pair pulled clear of the rest. The fact that Lezoo was able to reverse that form fairly comprehensively suggests that she had perhaps been unlucky in the earlier contest, especially as she was carried left by her rival, who had the race run to suit, in the closing stages. The September run also came after a break – she had four races in quick succession in June and July – and it looked to have done her the world of good. She's now fairly prominent in the betting for the 1,000 Guineas but the Commonwealth Cup over 6f at Royal Ascot may turn out to be a more suitable target for her as she looks more of a speedster than a miler. She's certainly one that Frankie Dettori will be eager to team up with again in his farewell season. RALPH BECKETT

LION OF WAR

3 b c Roaring Lion - Momentus (Montjeu)

Lion Of War was pitched in at the deep end following a comfortable maiden success at Leicester and a wide-margin novice victory on AW at Newcastle on his first two starts in June of last year. While he was far from disgraced in the Group 2 Superlative Stakes at Newmarket's July meeting, he failed to step up on the promise of those two wins. He again ran to a similar level in Listed company at Haydock in September and on his nursery debut at Doncaster (his first run on heavy) in October but, given he is a really imposing physical specimen, he might have been a bit on the weak side last year and it doesn't take much imagination to see him develop into a smart performer this season. His pedigree suggests he'll be well suited by the step up to at least 1m2f (he's by Roaring Lion out of a dam who stayed 1m4f) and he can exploit his current mark of 87 before going back into Listed and Group company. CHARLIE JOHNSTON

LITTLE BIG BEAR (IRE)

3 b c No Nay Never - Adventure Seeking (Bering)

Aidan O'Brien had a phenomenal year with his juveniles in 2022 with six of them winning Group or Grade 1 races, all of them with Ryan Moore in the saddle. Little Big Bear was the first of the six as he ran out a 7l winner of the Phoenix Stakes at the Curragh in early August, which earned him a RPR of 123, the highest rating achieved by a juvenile in 2022. He was supplementing earlier wins in the Listed Windsor Castle Stakes over 5f at Royal Ascot and the Group 3 Anglesey Stakes over an extended six furlongs at the Curragh, which he won by nearly 5l. Those wins propelled him to the head of the market for the 2,000 Guineas and, although he wasn't seen again, he's still there, although his stablemate Auguste Rodin, the winner of the Vertem Futurity Trophy in October, is now challenging him for favouritsm. The reason we didn't see Little Big Bear again was that he picked up a foot injury which ruled him out of the National Stakes in September and the Dewhurst in October. It was only a fairly minor injury however, likened to a similar issue as a human pulling off a fingernail, so hopefully his spring targets are not affected. An uncomplicated sort who races up with the pace, he looks certain to stay 1m on breeding so all the big Group 1s over that distance will be pencilled in. He has strong claims based on the evidence of his juvenile form. AIDAN O'BRIEN

LOCAL DYNASTY (IRE)

3 b c Dubawi - Really Special (Shamardal)

Local Dynasty's only defeat in four outings in 2022 came in the Group 3 Acomb Stakes at York's Ebor Festival on only his second start. While he proved disappointing on the face of it that day, the race worked out well with the winner Chaldean going on to land the Champagne Stakes at Doncaster and the Dewhurst at Newmarket in autumn, with a host of other winners emerging from further down the field. Charlie Appleby's colt quickly got back on track by winning a novice on soft ground at Sandown the following month, but he reserved his best effort for a Listed event at Pontefract in mid-October, where he showed a fine attitude to beat previous scorer Luckin Brewin by a neck, with subsequent Listed winner Caernarfon back in third. His jockey William Buick said: 'Local Dynasty saw that out well. He travelled through the race very easily and he really stuck his head out today. He has got a beautiful pedigree so there's plenty of hope for next year for him.' He has plenty in the way of physical scope and, assuming he improves further over the winter, it's not difficult to envisage this brother to a French 1m3f scorer developing into a minor Group winner over middle distances, especially when there is plenty of give in the ground. CHARLIE APPLEBY

LUDMILLA

3 b f Kingman - Rostova (Arch)

This filly created a favourable impression on her one outing as a two-year-old in 2022, which came in a 7f fillies' novice stakes on soft ground at Newmarket in October. She showed distinct signs of inexperience, running very green over 1f out before keeping on strongly in the closing stages to grab third close home. The form has yet to be properly tested but it could turn out to be a decent race of its type, with horses trained by Beckett, Balding, Varian, Haggas, Cox and Ferguson in opposition. A daughter of Kingman, she may have preferred a sounder surface in any case and it's distinctly possible that she will emerge as the best horse to come out of that contest. She ought to get off the mark in the early part of the turf season, possibly over 7f or a mile, and after that she's likely to find her niche as a handicapper over slightly further. JOHN & THADY GOSDEN

LUXEMBOURG (IRE)

4 b c Camelot - Attire (Danehill Dancer)

The unbeaten Vertem Futurity Trophy winner of 2021, Luxembourg was installed as the winter Derby favourite, but like so many horses trained by Aidan O'Brien he prepared for that race by running in the 2,000 Guineas at Newmarket in early May. Things conspired against him in that race, however, as he was short of room and stumbled at the start, and then, in a slowly run race, he was forced to make his challenge widest of all. He nevertheless kept on well in the closing stages to finish third behind the Godolphin pair Coroebus and Native Trail, who had essentially got first run on him. A step up in trip looked certain to suit and he unsurprisingly hardened to 5-2 favourite for the Epsom Derby on the back of the run. Sadly, he missed that race and a few other major summer meetings after sustaining a muscle injury and we didn't see him again until mid-August when he scrambled home by a neck from Insinuendo in the Group 3 Royal Whip Stakes at the Curragh over 1m2f. Again, a slow pace probably was against him and he actually did pretty well to outbattle the filly with his other four rivals all beaten a long way. He stepped up massively on that next time in the Group 1 Irish Champion Stakes, again over 1m2f, where he got the better of Onesto in a sustained battle in the final furlong with Vadeni, who had won the Prix du Jockey Club by a wide margin in June, a further length and a half away in third. He became one of the favourites for the Arc after that win but sadly he suffered another muscle injury during the race and he could only finish a staying-on seventh of twenty behind Alpinista, with Vadeni half a length behind the winner in second. O'Brien said afterwards: 'Luxembourg stepped awkwardly from the stalls and pulled a muscle coming out of the gates. He's a very brave horse, we've always seen that from him, and he put his head down and battled all the way to the line but he was very lame after the race.' However, it was also reported that he would stay in training as a four-year-old and O'Brien feels the best could yet be to come: 'We obviously didn't get a clear run with him this year so we hope that things will go a bit smoother next year.' AIDAN O'BRIEN

MAMMA'S GIRL

3 ch f Havana Grey - Mamma Morton (Elnadim)

A half-sister to Master Of War, a Listed winner for Richard Hannon in 2012, Mamma's Girl was well supported when making her debut in a fillies' novice stakes over 7f at Newmarket in October and she rewarded her backers by running out a comfortable winner. She has plenty of relatives who won at 1m and just beyond and Hannon thinks she may well return to Newmarket for the 1,000 Guineas in May: 'I thought she would be a Queen Mary horse but it was lovely to see her get the seven furlongs well after pulling pretty hard. She will be a lovely filly next year and she looks a Black Type filly. She will definitely get a mile and she could be a Guineas filly next year. She has won a Newmarket maiden well and though there are still options for her this year we could look at a Guineas trial next year for her.' Races like The Nell Gwyn Stakes and the Fred Darling Stakes will therefore be pencilled in for her in April and it will be interesting to see how she goes on from there. RICHARD HANNON

MANACCAN

4 ch c Exceed And Excel - Shyrl (Acclamation)

Based in one of the smaller yards at the bottom of Warren Hill in Newmarket, John Ryan has fewer than 20 horses in training but together with loyal owner Graham Smith-Bernal he has unearthed a bit of a diamond in the shape of this four-year-old, who won four races for him in 2022, including a Group 3 at Dundalk on his final run in October. A 100,000gns breeze-up purchase, Manaccan needed a bit of time to grow into his frame but he showed a fair bit of ability at two, including when finishing fourth in the Group 3 Cornwallis Stakes on his final start of the 2021 season. He improved steadily at three, notching his first win at the fourth time of asking in the Shergar Cup Dash at Ascot, where he edged out the veteran Judicial. He matched that when finishing third in a Listed race on the July course later the same month and he improved again by winning his first Listed race, the Scarborough Stakes at Doncaster, early the following month. He made a bold bid to follow up that win in a Group 3 over 5f at Newbury two weeks later but he lost out narrowly to Mitbaahy and Teresa Mendoza in a three-way dash to the line, having been forced to wait for a run about

2f out, which may have cost him the win. Another 5f Listed victory followed at Ascot in early October and he signed off for the season with that Group 3 win at Dundalk, where he won with more in hand than the half-length margin of victory would suggest. Based on his *Racing Post* Ratings he improved with just about every run at three and there are undoubtedly more Group races to be won this year. JOHN RYAN

MASO BASTIE

3 b g Churchill - Opportuna (Rock Hard Ten)

A gelded son of Churchill and a half-brother to two winners, Maso Bastie caught the eye on his debut in a 7f Kempton maiden in November which has already started working out well. Reluctant to load, he ran green throughout and became detached from the main bunch early on, but under considerate handling he made eyecatching late progress to finish fourth of the 13 runners behind Dagmar Run. One month later at Lingfield over an extra furlong he showed that he had learned plenty from that initial outing as he ran out a narrow winner from the far more experienced Miss Dolly Rocker, who is officially raced 74. As on his debut, he was fractious in the preliminaries and, having looked booked for fourth at best as they entered the final furlong, he suddenly went through the gears to get his nose in front where it mattered. His temperament is a concern of course, but there is plenty more to come from him if he goes the right way and he looks a useful prospect. JAMES FANSHAWE

MAUIEWOWIE

3 ch f Night Of Thunder - La Chapelle (Holy Roman Emperor)

Named after a variety of marijuana from Hawaii, Mauiewowie made an impressive winning debut in what turned out to be an above-average 5f Naas maiden in early July. Her trainer said afterwards: 'Mauiewowie is a filly we have liked. I'm not surprised she did that and here's hoping she can go on to be a Cheveley Park filly or something like that.' It was perhaps slightly disappointing in the context of that comment that she wasn't able to win a Listed race over the same C&D a few weeks later, but the horse who beat her, Lady Hollywood, would go on to win a Group 3 subsequently so it wasn't a dismal effort by any means. She bounced back to winning form in a 5f Listed race in August at the Curragh, getting the better of Treasure Trove near the finish with the third horse over 2l away. The runner-up would go on to win her next two starts, including a Group 3 at the Curragh, so, again, the form looks sound. Ger Lyons drew stumps on the season afterwards, saying: 'We'll see how she comes out of it but I wouldn't be surprised if you didn't see her again this year and we look after her until next year.' She looks sure to win Group races and she's one to follow. GER LYONS

MIDNIGHT MILE (IRE)

3 b f No Nay Never - Ruby Tuesday (Galileo)

Midnight Mile probably has to improve a fair chunk if she's to win the 1,000 Guineas, but she quickly made up into a smart performer in her first season of racing and she might be a live outsider for the first fillies' Classic if she progresses again through the winter. She was fairly easy to back before her debut at Doncaster in July but she posted an encouraging performance, overcoming greenness to beat Royal Dress, a rival who had the benefit of previous experience, with the pair coming clear of The Big Board, a subsequent winner. While that effort marked her down as a promising type, she stepped up appreciably on that form on her next outing in the Group 3 Oh So Sharp Stakes over 7f at Newmarket, where she kept on well to get up in the closing stages, shaping in the process as though a step up to 1m would suit. She ran over that trip on her next start in the Breeders' Cup Juvenile Fillies Turf but the tight turns of Keeneland proved against her and she could only manage a never-nearer fourth to leading filly Meditate, who had been placed in Group 1 company on each of her two previous starts. It's best not to judge Midnight Mile too harshly on that effort and she should be seen to better effect back in Britain in the coming months. Richard Fahey has won the Nell Gwyn twice since 2011 so expect to see her lining up in that contest before being allowed to take her chance in the Guineas, for which she's a 33-1 chance at the time of writing. RICHARD FAHEY

MILITARY ORDER (IRE)

3 b c Frankel - Anna Salai (Dubawi)

Even before he set foot into the paddock at Newmarket before his debut last October, Military Order took the eye on paper, being a full brother to 2021 Derby and King

George winner Adayar. There was a good deal of public support behind him at Newmarket but, although he kept plugging away in the closing stages in that 7f contest, he didn't have the pace to get to promising debut winner Enfjaar. Charlie Appleby lost little time stepping him up to 1m for his next outing back on the Rowley Mile just over two weeks later and he showed improved form, staying on strongly in the closing stages to beat stable companion and similarly promising sort Ancient Rules by three-quarters of a length in what looked an above average novice event. He was put away for the season after that win but, if he's anything like his illustrious sibling, he will be well suited by the step up to middle distances as a three-year-old. He has a long way to go before matching the achievements of Adayar, of course, but he couldn't be in better hands and he'll likely make up into a smart performer at the very least. He's only raced so far on good and good-to-soft ground. CHARLIE APPLEBY

MODAARA

4 b f Dubawi - Nahrain (Selkirk)

Modaara immediately takes the eye on pedigree given she's a sister to Saeed bin Suroor's globetrotting Benbatl, who won at the highest level in Australia, Europe and Dubai and retired with career earnings of nearly £6m. There have been several other winners to come from the dam, including this filly, who built on her debut promise at Yarmouth in September when successful at Chelmsford in late October. There was plenty to like about the way she got the job done, travelling strongly before pulling clear in the closing stages to beat a reliable yardstick in Idee Fixee – a horse that went on to post two solid efforts in defeat towards the end of the year. Although stumps were drawn for the season after that victory, she's open to a good deal of improvement this time round. She should stay a bit further than 1m2f and she can exploit a good-looking opening mark of 80 before going into better company. ROGER VARIAN

MODESTY (IRE)

3 b c Dubawi - I Am Beautiful (Rip Van Winkle)

There was nothing remotely modest about Modesty's impressive debut victory at York in October, and the three-year-old looks one to follow this season. This fourth foal of a 6f Group 2 winner seems to have much more in the way of stamina than his dam (who raced at no further than 7f), as he showed when winning over a trip just shy of 1m on ground described as good to soft, soft in places. He travelled really strongly and, although running green when initially asked for his effort, he soon grasped what was required and pulled clear in the closing stages to beat a 76-rated rival by three lengths. He wasn't seen out again but he looks a good prospect for 2023, with the step up to middle distances looking likely to suit. Only time will tell whether he's good enough to be competitive in a race like the Derby or the Irish equivalent (the yard's Lone Eagle finished a fine second to Hurricane Lane in that race in 2021) but, whatever the ceiling of his ability turns out to be, he's open to a good deal of improvement and seems sure to win a decent race or two along the way. FREDDIE & MARTYN MEADE

MOLAQAB

3 b c Zoustar - Saniyaat (Galileo)

A 150,000gns yearling, Molaqab showed enough on his sole outing of 2022 on the very last day of the Flat turf season to suggest that he has a bright future. He ran in a 6f maiden on heavy ground at Doncaster and it didn't start too well for him as he was slowly into stride before running green. Racing in last place, he got caught in traffic as they approached the two furlong pole and he then had to be switched left after being shaken up by his rider. Thereafter he ran on strongly to finish a never-nearer third of the nine runners, albeit several lengths behind the winner Tiriac. He should find plenty of improvement with that outing behind him and he's one to keep an eye on as he resumes his career at three. WILLIAM HAGGAS

MOSTABSHIR

3 gr c Dark Angel - Handassa (Dubawi)

A half-brother to dual Group 1 winning miler Nazeef and three-time Group 3 winner Mostahdaf, Mostabshir had an outside draw to contend with on his only start of 2022 in a 1m novice stakes at Kempton in November, but he got away well and was able to sit just off the early leader. Racing freely, he took it up two furlongs out and looked impressive as he drew clear in the closing stages to win by 4l from Davideo, who was having his second outing. It probably wasn't a strong race of its type but he could do no more than win and the time of the race was fairly decent. He looks a nice prospect. JOHN & THADY GOSDEN

MUJTABA

5 b g Dubawi - Majmu (Redoute's Choice)

Mujtaba was a shade disappointing in both the Lincoln and in the Cambridgeshire last season but, leaving those two ultra-competitive handicaps aside, he has a fine strike-rate and his record is largely one of progression. He didn't see the track as a juvenile but made up for lost time in his three-year-old season, winning all of his three starts and, given his profile, he looked an ideal type for last season's Lincoln. Things didn't work out that day and he was also beaten at Chester on his next start (though he ran respectably) but he got back on track when successful at Doncaster on the first day of a curtailed St Leger meeting, winning in fine style from his main market rival, Legend Of Dubai. The step back in trip on a sound surface didn't look to suit in the Cambridgeshire but he turned in easily his best effort when tackling heavy ground for the first time in his three-year-old season October, pulling clear in the closing stages to beat Fantastic Fox by seven lengths. Although the ground at Doncaster was officially 'good', It may be that testing conditions see him to best effect and, on this evidence, he'll be more than capable of making his mark in minor Group company when there's plenty of give underfoot. As he's only had eight starts, it's a fair bet that there's more to come and he's set for another productive season. WILLIAM HAGGAS

NATHANAEL GREENE

4 b g Nathaniel - My Special J'S (Harlan's Holiday)

Nathanael Greene's record last year was one of steady improvement until he came unstuck on his first start in heavy ground when down the field in the November Handicap at Doncaster on the final day of the Flat turf season. However, it's best to put a line through that Doncaster race given the demanding conditions and it's worth noting that he is otherwise fairly versatile regarding ground and trip given that he won over 1m2f on quick ground on his reappearance and over 1m6f on soft ground at Haydock in July. He was fitted with cheekpieces for the Haydock run and he matched that effort when fourth to Post Impressionist after a break of over three months in October, prior to the below-par Doncaster effort. He's not fully exposed yet and he's just the type his capable handler will eke further improvement out of this time round. He should win a decent middle-distance handicap. WILLIAM HAGGAS

NINE TENTHS (IRE)

3 b f Kodiac - Covetous (Medaglia d'Oro)

William Haggas's runners usually improve a fair bit for their debut runs and that was certainly the case with Nine Tenths, who did show distinct promise when fourth of ten on heavy ground at Doncaster (6f) in early November. This sister to a Spanish winner up to 7f out of a 7f winner turned in a much-improved display on her AW debut in the middle of that month when beating subsequent winner Cariad Angel in comfortable fashion, the pair drawing clear of the rest of the field. Although she hasn't been seen since, she appeals as the type to hold her own in handicap company before possibly going up in grade. Her dam won over 7f on soft-to-heavy and also seemed to stay 1m so the three-year-old should prove equally effective if and when she's stepped up in distance. She's a nice prospect. WILLIAM HAGGAS

NOBLE STYLE

3 b c Kingman - Eartha Kitt (Pivotal)

This 525,000gns Kingman colt was Charlie Appleby's first juvenile runner in 2022 and he didn't disappoint as he ran out a ready winner of a 5f novice stakes at Ascot in early May, beating Wallbank, Redemption Time and Royal Scotsman, who would all go on to win next time out. James Doyle said afterwards: 'That was a good performance, wasn't it? Noble Style hasn't done a huge amount of fast work at home but I know that what he had done had pleased everyone. He showed a good change of pace and he's from a fast family that's done well here before, so it's a promising start.' Having missed Royal Ascot because of an unsatisfactory blood sample, he probably didn't have to improve much to win again on his return to action three months later, this time in a 6f contest at Newmarket where he saw off Mill Stream and Wallop, with that trio pulling clear of the remainder. He next took on Marshman in the Group 2 Gimcrack Stakes and he defended his unbeaten record, beating that rival by a length and a quarter with a further five lengths back to Cold Case, who would go on to win his next two starts. He was expected to run in the Middle Park Stakes after that but a bout of colic intervened, forcing him to miss that engagement. However, Appleby confirmed in October that he had made a full recovery, saying: 'He's put away for the winter and is fine now and he's going to be that exciting horse in the spring that goes into those trials not knowing what level he is going to achieve.' CHARLIE APPLEBY

NOSTRUM

3 b c Kingman - Mirror Lake (Dubai Destination)

Whenever Sir Michael Stoute has a winning newcomer, it's a fair bet they turn out to be pretty good, and ready Sandown debut winner Nostrum confirmed he was smart when winning a Group 3 at Newmarket on his next start in September. That day, he proved far too strong for proven Group performer Holloway Boy, who went on to give the form some substance when placed in both the Autumn Stakes and in the Vertem Futurity Trophy. Nostrum was made 5-2 joint favourite for the Dewhurst on the strength of those two victories but, although he matched the form of his previous win, it was a surprise that he couldn't do better than a third placing to the same owner's Chaldean, who is trained by Andrew Balding. That run, only 16 days after his Group 3 win, could conceivably have come too soon and, given his imposing physique, it's not out of the question that he may need a bit more time to grow into his big frame. In fact, his trainer stated after the Dewhurst: 'Nostrum wasn't good enough today but he's a big scopey horse with a great mind on him. I haven't really thought about what next year might hold for him, but he'll have no problem getting a mile.' This half-brother to several winners up to 1m4f could easily leave those bare facts behind this year and he is well worth another chance to prove himself at the top level. It's not difficult to envisage him running well in a Guineas, whether it be at Newmarket or the Curragh. SIR MICHAEL STOUTE

NOVAKAI

3 b f Lope de Vega - Elasia (Nathaniel)

Karl Burke knows what it takes to have a credible 1,000 Guineas contender on his hands, having saddled Laurens to finish second to Billesden Brook in the 2018 renewal. Although Novakai hasn't achieved as much as that multiple

Group 1 winner at this stage of her development, she progressed through the ranks last year and looks the type to make her mark in Pattern company this time round. But, back to the start. The daughter of Lope de Vega created a fine impression on her debut over 7f at Doncaster in July when beating Crackovia, a subsequent winner in ready fashion, a performance that marked her down as one to note, even in stronger company. She was duly upped in grade for her next start and, although unable to justify favouritism, she stepped up on that debut form when a respectable fifth in the Group 3 Sweet Solera Stakes on the July Course at Newmarket in early August. But the step up to 1m proved a good move as she raised her game again when mugged by Polly Pot in the May Hill at Doncaster (a race, incidentally, that Laurens also won) in September. Her best performance was reserved for her final start when she gave the unbeaten Commissioning a bit of a scare in the Group 1 Fillies' Mile. She went down by a length but was a fair way clear of her stable companion Bright Diamond, who had been placed in a Group 3 on only her second start. She'll need a further step forward if she's to reverse placings with the aforementioned Gosden runner in the first Classic, but she is capable of better and 25-1 makes a bit of each-way appeal. Her pedigree suggests she'll be equally effective over 1m2f and she's one to look forward to. KARL BURKE

ORCHID BLOOM

3 gr f Farhh - Fire Orchid (Lethal Force)

This 55,000gns first foal of a seven-furlong AW two-year-old winner made an impressive winning debut over 7f at Newmarket in October on her only start as a juvenile. She came under pressure before a few of her rivals but she responded well and seemed to relish the soft ground, drawing away on the climb to the line to win by over 3l in a quicker time than the winner of the first division of the same fillies' novice. It's hard to know what to make of the form but she was in a different class to her opponents and one or two of them have already run good races in defeat since. She is the type to do better this year and she can make her mark in handicaps at around a mile. WILLIAM HAGGAS

PADDINGTON

3 b c Siyouni - Modern Eagle (Montjeu)

More was clearly expected from this 420,000euros yearling when he finished only fifth of eight on his debut in an Ascot maiden over 7f in early September. Having run green, Ryan Moore was pushing and shoving from about three furlongs out and he was struggling soon after. He eventually finished eight lengths behind the winner, City Of Kings, and at that stage entries in the Irish Guineas and English/Irish Derbies appeared rather fanciful. Six weeks later he ran in another 7f maiden, this time at the Curragh, and he had clearly improved massively from that initial outing as he ran out a five-length winner of that 20-runner contest, despite still showing signs of greenness. Aidan O'Brien said afterwards: 'We were disappointed with Paddington at Ascot – he was very green – but we gave him time and he came back. He always showed a little bit of class and we're delighted with that. He could start in a Guineas or Derby trial next year, possibly a Guineas trial, and we'll see then.' AIDAN O'BRIEN

PHYSIQUE (IRE)

3 b g Kingman - Shapes (So You Think)

A 170,000gns yearling, Physique made his debut in late October on rain-softened ground over 6.5f at Newbury and he very much caught the eye. Travelling sweetly in a prominent position, he took up the running over 1f out and he looked all set to make a winning debut before lugging left under pressure, thus opening the door for Novus, a more experienced rival, to just pip him at the post, with the pair clear of the third. Just one week later he ran over 7f at Newmarket, where he made all and didn't have to be ridden too vigorously to comfortably see off the Charlie Appleby-trained Majestic Pride by nearly two lengths. The third placed horse was a further six lengths away in third and the time of the race was over a second quicker than the other division of the same novice. Moreover, the runner-up boosted the form a few weeks later by easily winning a Chelmsford contest over the same trip. Physique looks useful on that evidence and he's one to look forward to – he could turn out to be Pattern class. PAUL & OLIVER COLE

POKER FACE (IRE)
4 b g Fastnet Rock - Stars At Night (Galileo)

Pontefract punters were treated to a plethora of promising performances at their 17 October fixture last year. Harry's Halo and Local Dynasty, who both figure in these pages, won the novice and the Listed race respectively but Poker Face also created a fine impression when bolting up in the 1m2f handicap, a performance which prompted the handicapper to raise him by a whopping 14lb. The rain-soaked ground conditions might have led to the exaggerated winning distance but he deserves credit given he failed to settle in the first half of the race on that handicap debut. That took his record to 3-3 after he'd won his first two starts at the same venue on his debut (good ground) in September and on Tapeta at Newcastle at the end of that month. His jockey at Pontefract, James Doyle, stated: 'You'd have to be impressed with that. They were obviously different conditions today than Poker Face has faced before but he's coped with them really well. Once the race settled down he relaxed beautifully and he quickened up well. He's progressing into quite a smart horse.' A smart horse indeed and, although he wasn't seen again after that quickfire three-timer, he's one who looks ready for Listed or minor Group company. It remains to be seen whether he'll be as effective on fast ground but it's a fair bet that there's more to come and, given he's essentially unexposed, he's one to look forward to this season. SIMON & ED CRISFORD

PRAKASA
4 b f The Ghurka - Khor Sheed (Dubawi)

Prakasa looks just the sort who could develop into a smart middle-distance filly for Roger Varian this season. This daughter of The Gurkha is related to several winners from 6f to 1m6f (notably the same owner's Listed and Group 3 winner Without A Fight) and, although she failed to justify favouritism on her debut, she shaped with plenty of encouragement when second to Pretending at Southwell (1m3f) in August. That experience was clearly not lost on her as she showed improved form to get off the mark at Kempton over a similar trip on her next outing where she was far too good for Sobegrand and market leader Beny Nahar Road. Although down markedly in distance with the hood removed for her final outing at Redcar (1m) after a short break in October, she deserves credit for filling the runner-up spot again, just in front of a subsequent winner in Compliant. The return to middle distances will suit, she's open to improvement and she should be able to make her mark in handicaps before going on to tackle Listed or minor Group company. ROGER VARIAN

PROSECCO

3 ch f Gleneagles - Elbereth (Mount Nelson)

A 110,000gns yearling out of a 107-rated Listed winner also trained by Andew Balding, Prosecco very much looked in need of the experience when she lined up for a 1m fillies' novice at Yarmouth in October. Weak in the market, she was having to be niggled along by Ryan Moore in the early part of the race and she then ran green about 3f out as she threatened to lose touch with the leading bunch. She then hung left under pressure over a furlong from home before finally getting the hang of things in the closing stages, finishing with real purpose to be beaten by only 4l by Bridestones. She may well have finished second had she not been forced to make her challenge widest of all while all the main action unfolded on the near side, with the winner taking full advantage of being up against the rail. Prosecco's dam was a winner over 1m4f and a step up in trip will no doubt see her in a better light at three. She can win her maiden at around 1m2f and she may also benefit from racing on slightly quicker ground – her debut came on going officially described as soft but her trainer had taken the filly out of an intended engagement earlier the same month at Nottingham with the same going description, citing the soft ground as the reason. ANDREW BALDING

QUEEN MAEDBH (IRE)

3 ch f Gleneagles - Euthenia (Winker Watson)

Having made a favourable impression in a barrier trial in early July, Queen Maedbh made her debut for Gavin Cromwell a week later in a 7f Leopardstown maiden where she confirmed that impression. Racing keenly, she took a while to respond to pressure as she was still a bit green, but she ran on strongly in the closing stages to finish within three quarters of a length of the Joseph O'Brien trained Montesilvano, who was having his second run. Two lengths away in third was Wave Machine, who boosted the form a few weeks later by winning a strong-looking maiden at the Curragh. Afterwards, the Gleneagles filly changed hands and her new owners switched her from Cromwell to Joseph O'Brien. Less than four months later she had her first run for her new connections and she won that 6f maiden at Dundalk in the manner of a decent filly, cruising through to lead over 1f out and quickly sealing matters to win by nearly three lengths from Catherine Of Siena. That rival would go on to win her next two starts, including a 5l romp over the same course and distance the following week, so the form looks decent. O'Brien's assistant Brendan Powell said afterwards: 'She is very relaxed at home so it's hard to gauge what she is but she showed a lot of speed here.' On pedigree she would appear capable of staying 1m (she has an Irish Guineas entry), but she may be kept to slightly shorter trips in the short term. JOSEPH O'BRIEN

RAINBOW SKY

3 ch f Sea The Stars - Best Terms (Exceed And Excel)

A sister to Star Terms, who was a Listed winner for Richard Hannon over 1m4f in 2019, Rainbow Sky was sent off a short price to make a winning debut when she lined up for a novice stakes over a mile at Kempton in November. However, she looked unlikely to justify those odds for much of the race, running green and getting outpaced early in the straight before eventually everything kicked into gear late and she finished strongly to get up by three quarters of a length from Urban Decay. The filly, who cost 1,500,000gns as a yearling, is open to any amount of improvement with that experience behind her and she's one to look out for as she resumes her career. CHARLIE APPLEBY

RESOLUTE MAN

3 ch c Dubawi - Lady Momoka (Shamardal)

Sheikh Mohammed Obaid Al Maktoum's homebred Resolute Man made his debut over 7f at Yarmouth in October and he created a favourable impression, winning by a length from Goodfella after travelling strongly and always looking in command in the closing stages. The form of that race has already started working out well with the second, third, fourth and sixth all achieving *Racing Post* Ratings in the mid-80s subsequently. Resolute Man, who has a middle-distance pedigree, looks a smart prospect for his owner-breeder as he steps up to 1m2f and beyond at three. He looks sure to win more races. ROGER VARIAN

ROYAL ACLAIM (IRE)

4 b f Aclaim - Knock Stars (Soviet Star)

Such was the promise of Royal Aclaim's first three runs (all wins), her season turned out to be a bit of an anti-climax following defeats in the Group 1 Nunthorpe at York and in a Group 3 in France on her final start. Nevertheless, she's an unexposed sort who has already achieved a high level of form and she's the type to make her mark in Pattern company in the coming months. James Tate's filly had only been seen once in 2021 (when winning at Newcastle in May of that year) but she stepped up considerably on that form when bolting up in a 5f novice at Bath on her first run for over a year in June. Her best effort was reserved for a Listed event at York four weeks later and she created a fine impression, travelling really strongly and coming home two lengths clear of Mondammej. On the strength of that, she started favourite for the Nunthorpe but she failed to build on that form, though she was anything but disgraced in sixth place behind Highfield Princess, who followed up in Group 1 company at The Curragh in September. Tate reported: 'It was probably not the best part of the track to be on but we're still a little bit disappointed. But it's only the fourth run of Royal Aclaim's career so I'm sure we'll keep moving forward.' Soft ground may well have been the reason that Royal Aclaim underperformed in France in September and she'll be well worth another chance back on a sound surface. She has only raced over 5f so far but she is well worth a try over 6f at some point. The Abernant over that trip at Newmarket in April could be an ideal starting point for the season. JAMES TATE

ROYAL DEESIDE

3 b g Churchill - Ebb (Acclamation)

Royal Deeside is one of Alan King's lesser-known horses at this stage of his development, but that could well be a different story come the end of the Flat season. The son of Churchill has only had three runs so far but he's shown promise at an ordinary level in each of those runs and he's the type to improve once he steps into handicap company.

He shaped as though a stiffer stamina test was needed when fourth of five on his debut at Ffos Las (7f) in August but he didn't initially improve for the step up to 1m2f, finishing only seventh of nine over 1m2f on good-to-soft at Goodwood after a short break in September. He posted a much better effort back on a sound surface on his final outing at Newmarket in October when fourth to Cannon Rock, form that has already been franked by the runner-up Sir Laurence Graff. Royal Deeside was gelded after that run and he'll be interesting in ordinary handicaps over middle distances from a mark likely to be somewhere in the low-to-mid 70s. Depending on how he fares this summer, it wouldn't be any surprise to see him figure over hurdles at some point later in the year. ALAN KING

SAN ANTONIO (IRE)

3 b c Dubawi - Rain Goddess (Galileo)

By Dubawi out of an Irish Oaks runner-up, San Antonio fared best of the newcomers when finishing fifth of ten runners in a 1m1f maiden at Tipperary in early October, with the race reader noting that he should improve plenty from the run. Two weeks later he ran in another maiden at Gowran Park, this time over a mile, and he duly improved by finishing third of the fifteen runners, having tried to make most. He only gave best close home and lost second place at the finish but it was a highly encouraging run in what looked a decent maiden. There should be plenty more to come from him over further at three – he should be able to shed his maiden tag in the spring and then establish himself over middle distances thereafter. AIDAN O'BRIEN

SEALINE (IRE)

3 ch c Australia - Zman Awal (Dubawi)

Given that Sealine is by Derby winner Australia out of a Dubawi mare who won up to 1m2f in Britain and Qatar, there's every reason to expect he'll be fully effective over middle distances this season. Roger Varian's colt started off over an extended mile on soft ground at Nottingham in August and he showed ability, staying on from off the pace to finish a never-nearer fourth behind Karl Burke's newcomer Liberty Lane. He hasn't been out since but he should be better for the run and there's a chance that a less testing surface should be more to his liking. He's open to plenty of improvement and, although he'll likely remain vulnerable against the better types in this grade, he should be able to make his mark in handicaps once he's qualified for an official rating. ROGER VARIAN

SISYPHUS STRENGTH

3 b f Sea The Stars - Childa (Duke Of Marmalade)

A 575,000euros half-sister to three winners including Group 3 winner Chilean, Sisyphus Strength came in for market support on her debut over 1m at Kempton in early September, but she missed the kick and ended up towards the back in a steadily run race, eventually finishing fourth. She did run on quite nicely in the closing stages and looked a likely improver, especially granted a stiffer test of stamina. Her next engagement was over the same trip at Nottingham at the end of the same month and she duly improved to score with a bit in hand. Her trainer upped her to Listed level for her final assignment of the year and she acquitted herself well, finishing fourth of ten behind Caernarfon in the Montrose Fillies' Stakes at Newmarket, again over 1m but on soft ground for the first time. Plenty went against her too – she raced keenly, then was hampered and she became unbalanced in the dip, but she still managed to grab fourth near the finish, with the front three too far clear of her to allow her to make any serious inroads on them. Her breeding suggests that a step up in trip will benefit her and, with more improvement to come, she is one to look forward to over middle distances in 2023. ANDREW BALDING

SLIPOFTHEPEN

3 ch c Night Of Thunder - Free Verse (Danehill Dancer)

John Gosden won the Derby with Benny The Dip in 1997 and with Golden Horn in 2015, and he has more than a sporting chance of adding to that Epsom success with the King's Slipofthepen. Now operating as a joint trainer with son Thady, Gosden snr will have no doubt been delighted with the striking impression Slipofthepen created on his debut over a mile at Kempton in late November. He showed greenness from the outset, missing the break and racing keenly, but he picked up early in the straight in the manner of a quality colt and he quickened right away from the field in the closing stages, prompting jockey James Doyle to say: 'We forfeited a bit of ground at the start through greenness but fortunately Slipofthepen is a pretty smart horse. He travelled super through the race and he made up a fair bit of ground in a matter of strides. It was difficult conditions in the fog with the lights shining and hopefully he has a bright future.' Although the bare form is nothing out of the ordinary (the fourth and fifth both showed fair form in defeat next time), he should have learnt plenty from the experience and he appeals strongly as the sort to hold his own in much better company at three. He's 25-1 for the 2,000 Guineas and 20-1 for the Derby and, although plans are unclear at this stage, he's possibly worth a small investment for both, his pedigree suggesting that the step up to middle distances is likely to suit. He's a fascinating prospect. JOHN & THADY GOSDEN

SUMO SAM

3 b f Nathaniel - Seaduced (Lope de Vega)

Given the amount of stamina on both sides of Sumo Sam's pedigree, it's highly encouraging she was able to win on her debut over 7f at an undulating track such as Newmarket. That she did – albeit narrowly – but she appeals strongly as the type to leave those bare facts well behind as she steps up to middle distances and beyond this season. Her 12-1 starting price at Newmarket in early October suggested that connections were more hopeful than confident of a bold show and, although she became unbalanced going into the Dip, she showed a fine attitude to get the lead back close home. That form looks no more than useful at this stage but she's a sizeable filly - just the type who will make a fair bit of progress over the winter. Assuming she makes the requisite improvement, she could easily be aimed at one of the Oaks trials – the Musidora at York might suit – and it's not beyond the realms of possibility that she could even develop into a St Leger type given her pedigree. She has a long way to go before she'd merit her place in Pattern company, but the dream is very much alive at this stage. PAUL & OLIVER COLE

TAFREEJ (IRE)

3 b g Shamardal - Taqaareed (Sea The Stars)

A gelded son of Shamardal out of a 1m4f winner, Tafreej very much looked in need of the experience when finishing sixth of 12 runners in a 6f novice race at Haydock at the start of September. Having made his way into contention, he took

a blow from about 2f out and soon faded away, but there was plenty of encouragement to be drawn from the run. Two weeks later he stepped up considerably on that initial effort when finishing third of fourteen over the same trip at Newbury, in a race which has already started to work out fairly well. He was kept to the same distance again at Yarmouth in October and this time he ran out a convincing winner, running on strongly to beat Poseidon Prince and Dear Daphne by upwards of two lengths. The form has yet to be fully tested, although the third horse did boost the form by running well in a Leicester novice over the same trip later that month. Tafreej is a half-brother to a 5f winner but his dam is a sister to Oaks/King George winner Taghrooda and the impression he gives is that a step up to a mile or more will see him in a much better light at three.
WILLIAM HAGGAS

TAHIYRA (IRE)

3 b f Siyouni - Tarana (Cape Cross)

Dermot Weld had a poor 2022 by his own high standards with just 23 winners on the Flat at a strike-rate of 7%, but there were a couple of notable high points for him to savour too. One was Homeless Songs, who won the Irish 1,000 Guineas by five and a half lengths in May and the other was Tahiyra, who now heads the market for next year's fillies' Classics after impressively winning the Group 1 Moyglare Stud Stakes in September. There was two and a quarter lengths back to Meditate at the finish in that 7f contest and that runner-up would boost the form in no uncertain terms two starts later when running away with the Breeders' Cup Juvenile Fillies' Turf at Keeneland. Chris Hayes rode Tahiyra with the utmost confidence at the Curragh and what she produced when asked for her effort was of the highest order as she left the favourite trailing in her wake on the prevailing soft ground. Weld was ecstatic: 'Tahiyra did it very well. It was an excellent renewal of the race and she has beaten a multiple Group-winning filly. I was afraid it might come a little soon in her career and I have always said she will be a beautiful filly next spring. We have a lot to look forward to.' Tahiyra is a half-sister to the stable's Tarnawa, who improved with age and there's every chance that there is plenty more to come from this filly too. Tarnawa won Group 1s at 1m2f and 1m4f but it looks like the Irish Guineas, won by her stablemate in 2022, will be the initial target, after which an Oaks will surely come under consideration. DERMOT WELD

TAJ NEOM (IRE)

3 gr g El Kabeir - Anythingknappen (Arcano)

A gelded half-brother to Italian 5f winner Donna, Taj Neom came in for market support before his debut run in a 6f restricted novice stakes at Pontefract in mid-October and he almost justified that confidence by finishing a close second of 11 runners. He did really well in the circumstances as he dwelt as the stalls opened, ran green towards the rear and then edged to his left when making headway over 1f, eventually finishing a never-nearer second behind Harry's Halo, who had raced much closer to the pace throughout. He would have been in front in another 50 yards as he hit the line full of running. The winner, an unconsidered 28-1 shot, proved that victory to have been no fluke when following up in a better race at Doncaster on the final day of the Flat turf season just over two weeks later, so the form looks more than okay in retrospect. Taj Neom should have learned plenty from that initial outing and the grey looks more than capable of winning races at three. KARL BURKE

TARAWA (IRE)

3 b f Shamardal - Tanoura (Dalakhani)

The Aga Khan's studs have been producing good quality winners for several decades and Tarawa looks the sort who could get some Black Type in her three-year-old career given she's by top sire Shamardal out of a good family that has produced Group 3 winner Taniyar and dual Group 3 winner Tanaza. Although unable to justify her position at the head of the market, she shaped well over 1m at Cork on debut in early September in a race that threw up winners. She bettered that effort on her only other run when dropped back to 7f at Leopardstown 45 days later, keeping on strongly in the closing stages to beat the Donnacha O'Brien-trained newcomer Bold As Love by two and a quarter lengths. That marked her down as a potentially smart sort and one that currently sits as fourth-favourite with one firm in the Irish 1,000 Guineas ante-post lists. She's got a long way to go before she can match the achievements of her owner's Tahiyra (also trained by Weld), who is clear favourite for that race after her impressive win in the Group 1 Moyglare Stud Stakes, but she appeals strongly as the sort to hold her own when her excellent trainer decides she's ready to mix it in Pattern company. DERMOT WELD

TONY MONTANA

3 b c Kingman - Mischief Making (Lemon Drop Kid)

'A winner waiting to happen' is how the *Raceform* race reader described Tony Montana after he had finished second behind Bluestocking in a strong-looking novice over a mile at Salisbury in late September. Held up in rear, he made eyecatching headway two furlongs out before running green, but he still looked like the likeliest winner as they entered the final half furlong. At that point Bluestocking came through with an irresistible surge against the far rail and Tony Montana had no answers but he still finished nicely clear of the third with seemingly plenty left in the tank. The horse who finished third was Racingbreaks Ryder, who would go on to boost the form by winning a similar race at Brighton two weeks later. Tony Montana has a Derby entry and he will be seen to better effect over longer trips as he resumes his career at three. Presumably a maiden over 1m2f or thereabouts will be on the agenda in the early part of the season, and if all goes to plan we can then expect to see him in one of the Derby trials. JOHN & THADY GOSDEN

TORITO

3 b c Kingman - Montare (Montjeu)

Group 1 winner Journey took five attempts before getting off the mark, and connections will be hoping it won't take as long to get her half-brother Torito into the winners' enclosure judged on his encouraging debut effort in novice company at Newbury in October. Given his pedigree and the fact he's housed in one of the best yards around, it was no surprise that he went off as the 11-8 favourite in a field of 14 but he shaped as though the run was just needed in the soft conditions, fading late having held every chance in the last furlong. The son of Kingman should have learnt plenty from that initial experience and it will be fascinating to see a route mapped out for him this season. It doesn't take much imagination to think he'll develop into a Pattern-race performer over middle distances (and possibly beyond) at some point and he's yet another from this powerful yard to look forward to over the coming months. JOHN & THADY GOSDEN

TRILLIUM

3 b f No Nay Never - Marsh Hawk (Invincible Spirit)

A No Nay Never half-sister to a couple of winners from 6f to 8.5f, Trillium made quite a pleasing start to her career in June when second of four in a 6f Goodwood maiden in which she was the only newcomer. Richard Hannon admitted later in the season that he was amazed she didn't win but she didn't look back afterwards. She got off the mark the following month at Newbury when she won a similar event by 4l from a host of future winners, including the fourth-placed Swingalong, who would go on to take the Lowther Stakes later that summer. Her next assignment was the Group 3 Molecomb Stakes at Goodwood, which is over 5f, and she took the drop in trip and rise in class in her stride as she easily got the better of Rocket Rodney and Walbank. Her best run of the season came in the Group 2 Flying Childers Stakes, also over 5f, at Doncaster in September, where she edged out the front-running The Platinum Queen in the manner of a very smart filly. The pair finished four and a half lengths ahead of Crispy Cat in third and the runner-up would go on to boost the form next time out by winning the Group 1 Prix de L'Abbaye at Longchamp. She was upped to 6f again on her final start, the Group 1 Cheveley Park Stakes at Newmarket in October, but it was her failure to settle rather than the extra furlong that cost her as she trailed in eighth of the ten runners behind Lezoo. She's clearly much better than that and she's a filly to remain interested at three. She's entered in the Irish 1,000 Guineas but perhaps sprinting will be her game and she could emerge as a contender for races like the Commonwealth Cup or July Cup in the summer. RICHARD HANNON

TUNNES (GER)

4 ch c Guiliani - Tijuana (Toylsome)

The German-trained Tunnes gets an entry in these pages given that he could easily turn up in one of the big middle-distance events in this country this summer – just like his half-brother Torquator Tasso did last season when chasing home Pyledriver in the King George at Ascot in July. There's plenty of similarity with his illustrious Arc-winning sibling given he's a progressive sort who goes particularly well with plenty of give in the ground. He notched his first win at the highest level (at the first attempt) when powering clear in the mud to win at Munich in early November. Admittedly the competition that day wasn't overly strong, but he created a fine impression, dictating a modest gallop before pulling clear in the last quarter mile. In hindsight a tilt at the Japan Cup later in the month probably wasn't the best move given it was on much quicker ground around a tighter track and he didn't have the pace to get involved, finishing just a respectable ninth of the 18 runners. However, he's the type to step up again this time round and conditions are bound to be more in his favour for a European campaign. He won't have to improve too much to get into the Arc picture and he will be a danger to all if there's plenty of juice in the ground, especially if he's allowed his own way out in front. PETER SCHIERGEN

UMBERTO

3 b c Expert Eye - Maria Letizia (Galileo)

There was some notable early market support for this half-brother to a 1m2f winner before he made his debut in a novice over a mile at Kempton in mid-November, and it was not misplaced as he ran a mighty race, finishing second, beaten a head by Like A Tiger, who was having his third start. Umberto, who raced prominently, made his challenge over 1f from the finish – a protracted duel with the eventual winner ensued and, while he made that rival pull out all the stops, he narrowly had to concede best in the closing stages, although, to his credit, he kept trying. There were over three lengths back to the third horse and just behind that one in fourth was God Of Fire, who gave the form a significant boost when running out a two-length winner of a Wolverhampton maiden a few weeks later. Umberto is bound to improve from that run and looks a certain winner as he resumes his career, perhaps over slightly further. KEVIN PHILIPPART DE FOY

VALUE ADDED

3 b f Iffraaj - Star Value (Danehill Dancer)

Although beaten a neck at Newbury on debut in heavy ground in October, the performance of the King's Value Added suggested that she could make up into a smart sort on better ground this coming season. A sister to a 1m winner with plenty of stamina on the dam's side of her pedigree, she caught the eye travelling really strongly before only just getting outpointed in the closing stages by the Andrew Balding-trained Opera Forever, who had the benefit of a previous run. Value Added is entitled to improve a fair bit for that run and she may be seen to better effect over 1m2f on less-testing ground this season. Trainer Richard Hughes will no doubt be keen to get a win out of her for the new monarch and a win in maiden or novice company should be a formality before she goes up in grade. RICHARD HUGHES

WANDERING ROCKS

4 ch g Ulysses - West Of The Moon (Pivotal)

If a line can be drawn through his disappointing last run at Doncaster, for which he has a valid excuse on account of unsuitably heavy ground, Wandering Rocks has a steadily progressive profile and he's just the sort to improve again for James Fanshawe this season. He showed improved form to win a Doncaster novice on only his third start in late July and, although he didn't add to his tally after that, he matched that form on his next run at Kempton before bettering it slightly back on turf at Newbury in September when third of ten behind Sam Cooke over 1m4f. His rating was left unchanged following that run and it's one he can take advantage of in the first few months of the new season. His style of racing (as with many from this yard) means he'll likely need a good gallop to be seen to best effect but he should be able to bag a handicap or two should things fall his way. JAMES FANSHAWE

WATERVILLE (IRE)

4 b c Camelot - Holy Moon (Hernando)

Horses like Yeats, Fame And Glory, Leading Light, Order Of St George and Kyprios have given Aidan O'Brien a high standing as a trainer of 'Cup' horses this century, with each of that quintet winning the Ascot Gold Cup in the last 15 years. Could he have another candidate for that race this year or in future years in the shape of Waterville? A massive horse, this half-brother to the Arc runner-up Sea Of Class started his career slowly in 2022 and he was being called some names after being beaten at odds-on in all of his first three starts in April and May. However, those runs were over 1m2f and 1m4f and when he was stepped up to 2m1f when contesting his first handicap at Limerick in June he looked a different proposition, winning comfortably. Surprisingly he was dropped back to 12.5f for his next start at Leopardstown in July and, try as he might, he couldn't quite get past the Joseph O'Brien-trained Point King, although that rival would win a Listed contest on his next start to give the form a boost. His next assignment was the Irish Cesarewitch over 2m124y in September and he did remarkably well to win that contest from Echoes in Rain, given that he was repeatedly denied a run between 3f and 2f out. He kept on strongly, however, to deny some far more battle-hardened rivals and Aidan O'Brien promised that there would be even better to come from him at four: 'Waterville is a massive horse and next year he's going to be something different. Over the winter he's going to turn into a different animal and he will be very much at home over Cup trips next year.' His final run of the season was a write-off as he finished last behind Trueshan in the Champions Long Distance Cup at Ascot (eased when beaten) but that was his seventh run of the season and perhaps it was one run too many. He's clearly much better than that and he can quickly make his mark at the highest level over two miles and beyond at four. AIDAN O'BRIEN

WEST WIND BLOWS (IRE)

4 b c Teofilo - West Wind (Machiavellian)

Despite a marked tendency to race freely, this son of Teofilo won three races from six starts in 2022 and, if he can learn to settle better, he still has plenty to offer as a four-year-old this term. He won a Nottingham novice over 1m2f by 5l in May, keeping on well despite setting a relentless pace, and it was decided after that to allow him to take his chance in the Epsom Derby in June. He ran respectably in that, finishing ninth of the 17 runners behind Desert Crown, only fading out of it in the final furlong having raced prominently. Back in calmer waters over a slightly shorter trip, he then won a 1m3f Listed race at Hamilton in July by seven and a half lengths from Groundbreaker, who is a fair benchmark for that level. He won that four-runner contest despite again taking a keen hold but he didn't get away with it at Goodwood in the Group 3 Gordon Stakes over 1m4f later the same month, where he finished sixth, fading out of it in the final furlong after wandering around in the closing stages. He then ran in another Group 3 over 1m2f at Longchamp

in September and this time he settled much better as he ran
out a comfortable winner, having been held up in midfield.
At that point connections briefly considered a tilt at the Arc,
but those plans were ultimately shelved and his final start of
the year came in a Group 2 at Longchamp over 1m2f on Arc
weekend, in which he again failed to settle and ultimately
finished a respectable third behind Anmaat and Junko on
the softest ground he had encountered to date. He has yet
to fully prove that he stays 1m4f but once he learns how to
settle he can surely win more Group races over that sort of
trip in 2023. SIMON & ED CRISFORD

WESTOVER

4 b c Frankel - Mirabilis (Lear Fan)

After showing a decent level of form over 1m in his juvenile
campaign in 2021, this imposing son of Frankel started his
three-year-old season in the Group 3 Classic Trial over 1m2f
at Sandown in April and, despite racing keenly and running
green, he managed to win that contest by a short head from
Cash, with the promise of plenty more to come. He was
pitched into the Epsom Derby next and it's fair to say that
he was unlucky in that race, even though he finished nearly
three lengths behind Desert Crown. He was repeatedly short
of room between 2f out and 1f out and, when he finally did
get a clear run after being switched, the winner had already
flown and he had to settle for third place, just behind Hoo
Ya Mal. There was a yawning five-and-a-half-length gap back
to the fourth and, despite the defeat, it marked Westover's
arrival at the top table. His next start in the Irish Derby
cemented that position as he ran out a 7l winner of that Group
1 contest, with his new rider Colin Keane taking the race by
the scruff of the neck from about two furlongs out. Tuesday,
back in fourth, clearly didn't give her running and the form
has taken one or two knocks since, but to take any Group 1 by
seven lengths takes a seriously talented horse. Unfortunately
Westover could finish only fifth and sixth on his final two
starts of the season but there are plenty of excuses for both
of those performances. Firstly, he boiled over before the start
of the King George VI and Queen Elizabeth Stakes in July
and he was beaten by 18l in that contest after racing with the
choke out and, while he ran a much better race in the Arc, he
could only finish sixth of 20 behind Alpinista, beaten by seven
and a half lengths. However, the very soft ground would not

have suited him at all and Ralph Beckett, who confirmed that the colt would stay in training, said afterwards: 'I thought he ran close to his Irish Derby run, if not his Derby run, on ground which didn't play to his strengths and it was great to get him back on track and that close to what his best is. He's a big horse, he's been growing through the year as well and he should improve from three to four. He's come out of the race really well, I'm really pleased with him and the way he's come out of it. We haven't made any plans yet, but I'm sure we will.' RALPH BECKETT

WOR WILLIE

5 b g Mukhadram - Caterina De Medici (Redoute's Choice)

A big shell of a horse, Wor Willie won three times in 2022 but there's every chance he will be even better next year as he fills into his frame. He started with a victory in a 0-70 handicap over 1m6f at Thirsk in April, in which he beat Blistering Barney, who won his next start convincingly. Upped in grade, he struggled to see out 2m at York on his next outing before running a shade disappointingly over a trip just shy of 1m6f at the same track in June. He stepped up massively on that next time though, winning a Pontefract handicap in July by seven and a half lengths. He was then game when winning over the same C&D in August, especially as 1m4f is regarded as his minimum trip. His regular pilot Paul Mulrennan had his own way in front in that four-runner contest and was able to dictate the pace, but his stamina kicked in as they entered the stiff finish and he stayed on well. Now 11lb higher than for the first of those Pontefract wins, he ran another excellent race in third at Ayr on his final start of the season, this time over 1m5f. He promises to be an exciting horse for this coming season, with many big Saturday races over 1m4f–2m likely to be on the agenda for him. His trainer suggested that there would be more to come from him as a five-year-old, saying: 'He's 17 hands, he's a shell of a horse and he'll be a better horse next year.' MICHAEL DODS

YASHIN (IRE)

4 b g Churchill - Mirdhak (Dansili)

Although Yashin was seen six times in 2022, it's unlikely this imposing animal has reached his full potential and he's just the sort to win a good-quality handicap on good or softer ground this season. A son of Churchill, Yashin caught the eye over 1m on his reappearance, shaping as though he'd be seen to better effect when going up in distance (as his pedigree suggests). He duly showed improved form when stepped up to middle distances, winning his first two outings in handicaps in May over 1m4f and 1m2f. He proved disappointing on the quickest ground he tackled in the King George V Stakes at Royal Ascot, but there was a valid excuse given he finished stiff behind that day and he's unlikely to be risked on ground as quick this time round. He showed that form to be all wrong with respectable efforts at The Curragh and Leopardstown on his last two outings but, given his physical presence, he should be a stronger sort this season. 1m4f with a bit of give in the ground could be his optimum conditions and it wouldn't be a surprise to see him over hurdles at some point later in the year. JESSICA HARRINGTON

YOTARID (IRE)

3 br c Shamardal - Hadaatha (Sea The Stars)

A half-brother to 1m3f (AW)–1m4f (turf) winner Moshaawer, Yotarid shaped pleasingly against a more experienced rival on his debut at Newcastle over 7f in November. Racing fairly prominently, he went second as they approached the final furlong and he then kept on willingly without ever being able to challenge the Karl Burke-trained Flight Plan, who was a comfortable winner by just over two lengths. There was a yawning gap back to the third and a few of the horses who finished in behind have already acquitted themselves well subsequently so the form appears sound. Yotarid promises to be suited by a mile and further and seems sure to improve as he gains further experience. ED WALKER

INDEX

NOTES

NOTES

100 WINNERS
JUMPERS TO FOLLOW
2023-24

Companion volume to ***100 Winners: Horses to Follow - Flat***, this book discusses the past performances and future prospects of 100 horses, selected by Raceform's expert race-readers, that are likely to perform well in the 2023-24 jumps season. To order post the coupon to the address below or order online from **www.racingpost.com/shop**

Tel 01933 304858

ORDER FORM

Please send me a copy of **100 WINNERS: JUMPERS TO FOLLOW 2023-24** as soon as it is published. I enclose a cheque made payable to Pitch Publishing Ltd for **£7.99** (inc p&p)

Name (block capitals) ....

Address ....

....

Postcode ....

SEND TO: PITCH PUBLISHING,

SANDERS ROAD, WELLINGBOROUGH, NORTHANTS NN8 4BX